DEBATING
THE ISSUES

Genetic Engineering

Cavendish
Square

New York

**ELIZABETH
RICE**

Published in 2014 by Cavendish Square Publishing, LLC
303 Park Avenue South, Suite 1247, New York, NY 10010

Copyright © 2014 by Cavendish Square Publishing, LLC

First Edition

Website: cavendishsq.com

This publication represents the opinions and views of the author based on his or her personal experience,
knowledge, and research. The information in this book serves as a general guide only. The author and
publisher have used their best efforts in preparing this book and disclaim liability rising directly or indirectly
from the use and application of this book.

CPSIA Compliance Information: Batch #WW14CSQ

All websites were available and accurate when this book was sent to press.

Library of Congress Cataloging-in-Publication Data

Rice, Elizabeth.
Genetic engineering / Elizabeth Rice.
  p. cm. — (Debating the issues)
Summary: "Examines the two sides of the debate related to genetic engineering and each of their benefits
and dangers, including the implications in medicine, cloning, the environment, agriculture, and more"—
Provided by publisher. Includes bibliographical references and index.
ISBN 978-1-62712-413-3 (hardcover) ISBN 978-1-62712-414-0 (paperback) ISBN 978-1-62712-415-7 (ebook)
1. Genetic engineering—Juvenile literature. I. Title.
QH442.R52 2013
576.5—dc23
2011046117

Editor: Peter Mavrikis
Art Director: Anahid Hamparian
Series design by Sonia Chaghatzbanian
Production Manager: Jennifer Ryder-Talbot
Production Editor: Andrew Coddington

Photo research by Alison Morretta

The photographs in this book are used by permission and through the courtesy of:
Front cover: corfield/Alamy.
Alamy: Jason Smalley/Wildscape, 11; David Frazier/Corbis Premium RF, 20; Jim West, 24; Deco Images II,
32; Atli Mar/Nordicphotos, 40; Nigel Cattlin, 47; Frances Roberts, 50; Nick Cobbing/David Hoffman Photo
Library, 55. **Associated Press**: Ronen Zilberman, 25. **Getty Images**: Kazuhiro Nogi/AFP, 6; Henning Dalhoff/
Bonnier Publications, 8; 3D Clinic, 10; Matt Meadows, 14; Ted Spiegel/National Geographic, 22; David
Greedy, 27; Sam Yeh/AFP, 37; Agricultural Research Service, 52; Ted Thai/Time & Life Pictures, 54; Inga
Spence, 56. **Superstock**: Dave Reede/All Canada Photos, 1, 2-3, 4-5, 45; Mauritius, 13; Science Faction, 16,
30.
Back cover: Nick Gregory/Alamy.

Printed in the United States of America

Table of Contents

Chapter 1

"**A** rose is a rose is a rose," wrote Gertrude Stein in a 1913 poem. But is a rose still a rose if it contains blue pigment genes from a petunia? Is it a rose if it contains antifreeze genes from a fish? We have entered a new era where scientists have powerful state-of-the-art tools to alter living organisms. These tools, together with a growing knowledge of genetics, enable scientists to move genes from one species to another. Genetic engineers can also make genetic copies (clones) of an individual, repair a broken gene, and turn off a working gene. These techniques have potential to solve medical problems, increase crop yields, and clean up environmental disasters. However, just because scientists can do something does not mean that they should. The new genetic capabilities have leaped ahead of our legal and ethical decision making, leaving many difficult questions.

DNA Is DNA Is DNA

A cell is far smaller than the naked eye can see. Inside each one lies the complete recipe book for building an individual. The individual might be a mouse, a tomato, a bacterium, or a tiger, but the language in which each book is written is precisely the same. The book is the **nucleus**. The recipes are genes, and the language consists of chemical **DNA** bases, abbreviated with the letters A, T, G, and C.

Blue roses, developed in 2006, contain a blue pigment gene transferred from petunias.

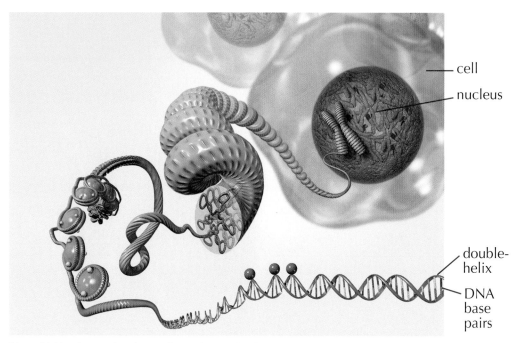

cell

nucleus

double-helix

DNA base pairs

Most DNA is housed in the nucleus of the cell. The paired DNA bases form a twisting double helix that supercoils in a condensed chromosome. Humans have 23 pairs of chromosomes.

The key to genetic engineering is that DNA works the same way in nearly all organisms. A cell reads, copies, and uses the DNA in precisely the same ways whether the cells belong to an elephant, a jellyfish, a peanut, or a virus. The only thing that identifies DNA as belonging to an elephant rather than a jellyfish is where it is housed. If DNA could somehow be moved from a jellyfish into an elephant, it would work in exactly the same way. In fact, scientists have moved a green florescent protein from jellyfish into a clear zebra fish and created a zebra fish that can glow green.

DNA REVIEW

DNA is found in the nucleus of nearly every cell. Cells also have small extra amounts of DNA in other structures, such as the mitochondria and chloroplasts. Regardless of location, all DNA works the same way.

Sections of DNA called **genes** encode **proteins**. Proteins are essential in life. Proteins are the fabric of muscles. Proteins are the enzymes that break down food. Proteins are the antibodies that defend a body against disease.

DNA is composed of repeating blocks. Each block has three parts: a nucleic acid, a sugar, and a phosphate group. The sugars and phosphates link to those of neighboring blocks to form a strong, flexible "backbone." The nucleic acids, also known as bases, are the A, T, G, and Cs that encode the genetic information. The nucleic acids pair with each other: A matches with T, and G pairs with C. The pairs of bases form the rungs of a twisting ladder, called the **double helix**. The double helix is a very stable way to store information because the information on one strand of DNA is backed up on the other strand. To use the information, an enzyme untwists the helix, separates the DNA strands, and reads or copies them to create proteins from the DNA.

DID YOU KNOW?

DNA is the same in nearly all organisms. It has the same building blocks and is used in the same way. Therefore, if a piece of bacterial DNA is transferred to a corn plant, the corn plant will make the protein encoded by the bacterial gene. By 2013, more than 65 percent of the corn planted in the United States contained a bacterial gene that repels insect predators.

Genetic Engineering

People have been making indirect changes to the genes of plants and animals for thousands of years through the process of **artificial selection**. When early farmers replanted the largest, heaviest seeds of the wheat harvest, they were intentionally changing the genes of the plants. When people breed cows for high milk production, sheep for thick wool, and dogs for hunting rabbits, they are using artificial selection to intentionally change the genes of animals. Plant and animal breeding, however, is not genetic engineering.

Like plant or animal breeding, **genetic engineering** is intentional, human driven, and goal oriented.

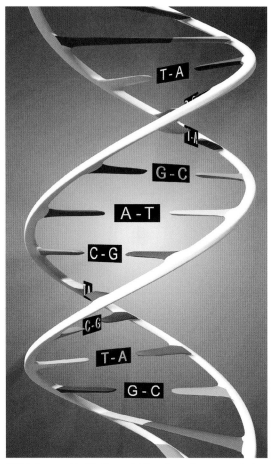

DNA bases (A, T, G, and C) pair to form a twisting double helix — a very stable way to store genetic data.

Genetic engineering, however, requires making direct, physical changes to the sequence of DNA in an organism.

DID YOU KNOW?

The term "genetic engineering" is older than our understanding of DNA! Jack Williamson popularized the term in his 1951 science fiction novel *Dragon's Island*. Scientists did not confirm the role of DNA in inheritance until 1952 or its double-helix structure until 1953.

Breeding cows for increased milk production using traditional cross-breeding and artificial techniques results in genetic modification but is not genetic engineering.

That sounds reasonably simple, but how do scientists make changes to such tiny particles? They cannot take scissors and clip out the jellyfish fluorescence gene. They cannot use tape or glue to stick it anywhere they want. Instead, genetic engineers use chemistry to copy, paste, and build new DNA.

Genetic engineering processes generally take one of three forms:

1. Finding, optimizing, and moving a gene.
2. Copying, or cloning, whole organisms.
3. Creating DNA from scratch.

Finding, Optimizing, and Moving

Nearly all genetically engineered products on the market fall into the first category. Find a gene that does something useful. Optimize by adding other genetic pieces and making copies of it. Move it to a new place, usually in a different species of plant or animal. It sounds straightforward, but each of those steps requires large amounts of time, money, and knowledge. For example, consider the zebra fish with the fluorescent protein from the jellyfish. First, researchers had to identify the trait they wanted: fluorescence. They chose jellyfish to investigate, but they might have chosen fireflies or any other green fluorescent organism. How did they find the actual DNA that encodes the flourescence gene? Jellyfish have millions, if not billions, of base pairs of DNA. They have thousands of genes. Finding a gene can take years.

Once researchers find the gene, they need to optimize it for best performance in its new host. They construct a genetic package by adding components like genetic switches to enhance protein production and marker genes to report successful transfer. Once the engineered gene construct is ready, copying it is relatively easy. The process takes advantage of an organism's natural ability to copy DNA and can happen inside or outside living cells, depending on the specifics of the engineering plan.

The hardest step, by far, is moving the gene into a new cell. Organisms and cells have powerful reasons to protect their DNA—changes, also known as **mutations**, can be dangerous. For decades, scientists struggled with finding effective ways to move DNA into new cells. Only a few organisms, such as viruses, have the ability to move DNA into another organism. To engineer animals, scientists often use adenovirus—a virus that causes colds and respiratory infections. To engineer plants, scientists often use a bacterium, *Agrobacterium tumefecans*, which in nature injects its DNA into oak trees, causing them to make tumors, also called galls. Another approach uses electricity to make short-term holes

The crystal jelly, *Aequorea victoria*, glows in the dark depths of the Pacific Ocean from Alaska to California. Scientists have isolated the fluorescent protein in the jellyfish's DNA and moved it into many other organisms, including zebra fish, monkeys, and mice.

GENE GUN

What does a plant breeder do if viruses or bacteria will not move DNA into the target plant? In the 1980s, John Sanford, a plant breeder at the Cornell Agricultural Research Experiment Station, faced this problem. In collaboration with other scientists, Sanford decided to shoot the DNA into the plant cells with a "gene gun." The first gene gun was an air rifle that used a plastic bullet coated with DNA particles. Some updated gene gun models look more like air compressors, while others have the appearance of futuristic pistols.

When the DNA-coated metal particles blast into the plant tissue, much of the tissue is destroyed. Around the smashed center is a ring of cells where the DNA has been driven into the nucleus. Once inside, the DNA can be incorporated into the chromosomes. Using the gene gun is technically easy (compared with using viruses or bacteria) and works for most plants. The DNA enters the nucleus of very few cells, however, and therefore tens of thousands of cells must be blasted in order to obtain a few successful ones.

A gene gun uses compressed air to blast metal particles coated with DNA into a cell's nucleus.

in membranes that allow DNA to enter the nucleus. Scientists can also use a gene gun to shoot DNA directly into cells.

Merely putting DNA into the nucleus of the destination cell is not success. When the new DNA enters the cell's DNA, it may insert itself into places where it destroys important genes, or it may not be incorporated at all. Occasionally, it goes into a place where the DNA is not copied and used. Sometimes so many copies go in that the plant shuts them down and will not make the protein. Only rarely do the right number of copies go into the right place to be transcribed at the right rate to produce the desired effect.

Because scientists need to screen many thousands of potentially engineered cells to find the "right" ones, they need a shortcut. Instead of looking at each individual cell, scientists move a marker gene along with the gene of interest. Marker genes can encode fluorescent proteins, colored proteins, and proteins for antibiotic resistance. This enables scientists to scan millions of engineered cells to find the few successfully engineered ones.

Creating Clones

In biology, cloning is the process of creating a genetically identical copy of a gene, a genetic sequence, or an individual. Scientists clone genes to learn about their structure and function. Cloning of whole individuals can occur naturally—identical twins are **clones**. Amoebas, sea anemones, and some plants have the ability to divide themselves into two, genetically identical individuals. This process is also called **asexual reproduction**.

DOLLY

In 1997, a sheep named Dolly grabbed headlines all over the world. Researchers in Scotland had succeeded in cloning an adult sheep by taking the nucleus from one of its cells and placing it into an egg cell from a different sheep. The developing egg was then implanted into a third sheep. After a normal pregnancy, Dolly was born. Dolly was a clone of the first sheep; the DNA in her cells was identical to the DNA in the nucleus removed from the adult sheep. The process started with 277 eggs. From these, 29 embryos developed. Only Dolly survived.

Dolly appeared normal; she gave birth to six lambs. However, she lived only six years, a relatively short life span for a sheep. She suffered from arthritis and died from a respiratory infection, unusual conditions for a sheep of her age. Many scientists point to Dolly and evidence from cloned mice, cows, and other animals to show that clones are often not healthy or long-lived, though the reasons are not fully understood.

Dolly the sheep was the first mammal cloned from an adult cell in 1997.

Genetic engineering has the potential to create clones of any organism. The most common way of cloning is to remove the nucleus, which contains all the DNA of an organism, from a cell. The nucleus is then placed into an egg cell that has had its own nucleus removed. By using hormones and other environmental cues, scientists can coax the egg through normal development.

Creating DNA from Scratch

For a long time, scientists have had the ability to use chemistry and enzymes to make stretches of DNA. In 2003, they succeeded in creating a living organism completely from scratch. The new organism is a virus—the simplest of living creatures. Some people argue that viruses are not actually alive because they cannot reproduce without a host. In 2007, the same group of scientists built a bacterial **chromosome** from

Organisms and Their Varying Amounts of DNA

Organism	Million base pairs (Mbp) of DNA	Predicted genes	Number of chromosomes (haploid)
Mycoplasm genitalium	0.58	485	1
Escherichia coli (intestinal bacteria)	4.6	4,200	1
Yeast (Saccharomyces cerevisiae)	12	5,800	16
Rice (Oryza sativa)	420	40,000	12
Human (Homo sapiens)	3,200	20,500	23
Onion (Allium cepa)	16,400	~40,000	16
Salamander (*Ambystoma tigrinum*)	26,900	~50,000	14
Fritillaria assyriaca	120,000	Unknown	12

scratch. They chose to work with one of the simplest known free-living organisms—a bacterium called *Mycoplasma genitalium*. The chromosome has 580,000 base pairs of DNA—the largest piece of DNA built at that time. The chromosome has a minimal set of genes required for life. In 2009, this artificial *Mycoplasma* chromosome was inserted into a living cell, where it then had the capability of guiding life. The human-created *Mycoplasma* can live, grow, and reproduce itself.

The Genetic Engineering Toolbox

The tools and techniques of genetic engineering are just tools—like a hammer or a sewing machine. Many scientists see genetic engineering as a simple extension of the selective-breeding process that humans have been using to shape plants and animals for thousands of years. Genetic engineering tools now allow scientists to cross species barriers and insert useful genes from one species into another.

Though conceptually simple, the steps of genetic engineering are technically difficult. Scientists are relatively skilled at finding and copying genes, though the processes can be time-consuming and expensive. Inserting desirable genes into cells is still a somewhat crude process that leaves a great deal to chance. As a result, scientists must screen thousands, even millions, of cells for the few with the desired effect. Once those cells are found, the traditional tools of selection are used to move the genes around within the species. The genetic cloning of humans and the creation of new organisms from scratch still remain more science fiction than fact, however. In reality, although scientists have managed to clone animals, the process has a low success rate and the clones often have poor health. Only very recently have researchers managed to create an entirely new functioning organism—a virus. While future genetic engineering opens the possibility of many technical feats, the ethical, legal, and regulatory issues of genetic engineering require immediate attention.

In and of themselves, the tools of genetic engineering are neither good nor bad. The challenge is in assessing how the tools should be applied.

WHAT DO YOU THINK?

Is it a good idea to make genetic changes in an organism? Does it matter if the "tool" for genetic change is natural selection, artificial selection (plant or animal breeding), or genetic engineering?

Is genetic engineering an extension of selective breeding processes? What are the similarities? What are the differences?

Is it a good idea to clone organisms? If so, which kinds? High-milk-production cows? A beloved pet dog? People? What are some of the problems with cloning?

Does it matter how people move genes into genetically engineered organisms? Are there health, ethical, environmental, or other important issues to consider?

What are the ethical, legal, and regulatory issues that scientists and society should consider as genetic engineering moves forward?

Chapter 2

The future holds many challenges for people and the land they live on. We are in the middle of a population boom. By 2050, experts expect there will be more than 9 billion people sharing this planet. That is nearly 30 percent more than the approximately 7 billion people on the planet now. There are an estimated 1.4 billion people without enough to eat now. How will we come up with 30 percent more food? We are already using nearly all the land on which food can be grown. Genetic engineering has some potential answers. It also has some potential solutions to medical and environmental problems currently without solutions.

Food: What Will We Eat?

Growing enough food to feed the world depends on the amount of land that people farm and how much food they can grow on that land.

DID YOU KNOW?

The current world population is close to 7 billion. The United States has a bit more than 312 million people, less than 5 percent of the world population. That proportion is not expected to change much. When the world population reaches 9 billion, the U.S. population is projected to be 400 million. However, the United States has more than 8 percent of the world's agricultural land.

Genetic engineering has the potential to boost crop yields in order to feed the world population of 9 billion people expected by 2050.

To feed more people, we need either more land or improved methods to produce more food from that land. Every year since 2001, the amount of land for growing crops has shrunk. Irrigation waters evaporate from agricultural fields. In many places the salt left behind has become toxic to plants. Other places have desertlike conditions because rich, nourishing topsoil has blown away with the wind or been washed away with the rain.

So how does the world feed ever-increasing numbers of people from lands that stay the same or decrease in size? Farmers, with help from scientists, have found ways to harvest more food from the same amount of land. Between 1950 and 2000, grain yields more than doubled, from 16.5 bushels per acre (1.1 tons per hectare) to 40.5 bushels per acre (2.7 tons per hectare). Some of these gains came from using oil-based chemicals such as fertilizers and pesticides. Some increases were the result of better land-management practices. Much of the gain is attributed to the varieties of plants being more productive. These plants were created without genetic engineering but with plenty of help from genetics and artificial selection. Farmers using artificial

Irrigation waters evaporating from cropland can lead to toxic accumulation of salt that can reduce or eliminate crop yields.

> **DID YOU KNOW?**
>
> How do species change with time? They change by selection. With *natural selection*, in each generation the most successful individuals produce the most offspring. Because these fit parents pass their genes for success along to the next generation, the "successful" genes increase in the population. Artificial selection has the same effect, except that human beings choose the genes that will be passed along to the next generation.

selection choose desirable individuals, whether they are wheat plants or cows, and using them as parents for the next generation.

The problem with traditional plant and animal breeding is that it usually requires sexual reproduction. Sexual reproduction changes gene combinations. The female offspring of a milk-producing cow will often not be quite as productive as the mother was. So scientists decided to turn to cloning. Margo, a two-year-old cow, broke milk production records. Surely, milk production would go up if more cows were just like Margo. In fact, Margo was cloned, and Margo II was also a very highly productive cow.

Cloned animals tend to live short lives for reasons not yet understood. Furthermore, they are often plagued by health problems, including poor immunity. A herd of genetically identical cows is especially vulnerable to disease. If a virus sickens one, chances are good that it will infect all the other cows—especially when they live in the close quarters of a barn or feedlot. In theory, a cloned cow will be exactly like her genetically identical predecessor. But in reality, there are differences. Even identical twins can be very different. The environment plays a role in shaping all individuals, even clones.

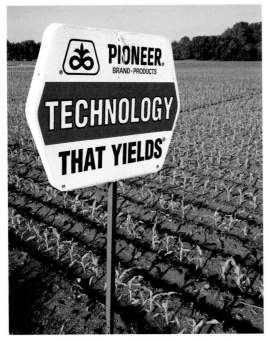

Hybrid varieties of corn more than quadrupled yields in the United States from 1930 to 1990 without genetic engineering.

Why do scientists not just engineer a plant that makes more food? The problem is simple: we need plants with high yield in order to produce more food on the same amount of land. Genetic engineering is good at moving single genes around. However, there is not just one gene that controls yield. In corn, dozens if not hundreds of genes control yield. The fact that they all interact with one another and the environment the plant is grown in creates a very complicated problem that genetic engineering is unlikely to solve alone.

However, genetic engineering has lots of solutions for smaller, more specific problems. It can produce plants that tolerate salty soils, lack of

HAWAIIAN PAPAYA

One of the first successful genetic engineering stories involves the papaya. Papaya plants are nature's clones. If you cut a branch off a papaya plant and put it in the soil, it will grow into a plant genetically identical to the first. In the Hawaiian Islands, papaya is the second most important crop, worth more than $45 million a year. Because whole plantations consist of genetically identical papaya plants, they are equally vulnerable to any disease or insect pest. The biggest threat in the past was papaya ringspot virus.

In the 1950s, the virus wiped out all the papaya production on the island of Oahu. Papaya production moved to Maui, an island that the virus had not reached. By 1992, the virus showed up in the papaya-growing area of Maui. By 1997, papaya production in Hawaii had dropped by almost 40 percent. Most papaya farmers have small farms so losing their crop can have devastating effects.

A plant scientist named Dennis Gonsalves had an idea. What if plants could be "vaccinated" against the virus in much the same way people are vaccinated to protect them against the polio or smallpox viruses? Unlike humans, plants do not have complex immune systems, however, and so it is amazing that this approach worked. Gonsalves took a gene from the virus that makes a "coat protein," meaning one that protrudes from the virus's exterior, and engineered it into a papaya plant. The plant soon produced the virus protein all by itself, and the virus could no longer infect it. (Why this worked is not well understood.) By 1999, the virus-resistant papaya varieties were increasing papaya production in Hawaii once again.

water, and heavy metals in the soil. What if some of the land lost to salt or creeping deserts could be reclaimed for farming? Perhaps the land could be reclaimed with plants engineered to live under salty or dry conditions. For example, in 2001 a tomato was engineered to live in salty soils. The genes inserted into this tomato variety pump salts out of cells and into storage areas called vacuoles. By storing extra salt in its leaves, the plant was able to thrive in soils fifty times saltier than typical tomato plants could. According to reports, the tomato tasted normal. Engineered plants have the potential to grow in lands too salty for crops today.

Increasing the nutritional value of some crops is another problem that genetic engineering can address. An estimated 1.4 billion people, more than 20 percent of the world's population, do not get enough to eat each day. Many of these people are women and children. Poor people tend to rely on grain because it is less expensive than other foods. Grain is not nutritionally well balanced, however. For example, roughly 40 million children do not get enough vitamin A in their diets. Vitamin A comes from green leafy vegetables, such as spinach, or from carrots, squash, and other orange vegetables. Grains contain very little vitamin A. Half a million children go blind every year because of a vitamin A deficiency. Some die. Many become sick because their immune systems cannot work properly. Malnutrition and the resulting lack of nutrients is a serious problem.

Genetic engineering of plants and animals has the potential to increase the amount of food available for the world's rapidly increasing population. One of the most common and arguably most successful applications of

GOLDEN RICE

What if people could get all the nutrition they needed from grain? Because rice is the most common staple crop in the world, in the 1990s Ingo Potrykus and Peter Beyer, with help from many others, created golden rice. Golden rice is regular white rice engineered with a protein from daffodils that the body quickly turns into vitamin A. Golden rice is indeed gold in color—it makes enough of the engineered daffodil protein to transform white grain into gold.

Golden rice was a technological triumph. The project was undertaken with the best of intentions: to use technology to help the world's poor and hungry. But is genetic engineering the best way to increase vitamin A intake? A 3.5-ounce (100 g) bowl of golden rice contains less than 10 percent of the U.S. recommended amount. Perhaps it would be cheaper, easier, and more effective to distribute vitamin capsules. There have also been regulatory and political problems with golden rice. Some consumers are unwilling to eat transgenic plants. Will people accustomed to eating white rice be willing to eat yellow rice?

"Golden rice" contains a daffodil protein that turns white grain into gold.

genetic engineering is modification of agricultural plants. Plants may be engineered to grow in dry or salty areas. Engineered plants may be able to deliver vitamins and minerals to hungry people who depend on grains. Generally, scientists create most of these new crop varieties by finding genes of interest, copying them, and inserting them into a crop of interest. Cloned animals, though produced by different genetic engineering techniques, may also be able to increase food supplies by replicating the successes of a few remarkably productive animals.

Medicine: What Will Make Us Well?

If agriculture represents one of the most common applications of genetic engineering, medicine represents one of the least successful applications. For the last twenty years, people have been predicting that our rapidly growing knowledge of genetics and genetic engineering

DID YOU KNOW?

What if you could deliver vaccines with a banana instead of a syringe? Every year 20 percent of infants are not vaccinated, resulting in 2 million preventable deaths a year. Injected vaccines need to be kept cold and used quickly to be effective. Therefore, vaccination is often most difficult in poor, rural communities of the developing world, where access is limited and refrigeration is scarce. Since 1997, clinical trials in humans and animals have shown that edible vaccines, engineered into plants, are a real possibility for delivering vaccines. Bananas have emerged as one of the best candidates, though potatoes, carrots, lettuce, and spinach have all been successfully engineered. Someday, a young child in a rural African village may be able to be vaccinated simply by eating some bananas.

will radically change medicine. So far, the change has not happened. There have been small success stories about the production of medicines for traditional approaches to healing, but the promise of major medical improvements remains on the horizon.

Our growing knowledge of the human **genome**—all the genes within an individual—is leading to much greater understanding of how altered genes can cause disease. These altered—some might say broken—genes will likely make good targets for medicines. A broken gene results in a loss of function; for example, a protein that does not do the job it is supposed to do. It is easy to imagine a medicine that could replace the missing protein. Replacement is already common in medicine without using genetic engineering. For example, many diabetics use insulin to supplement their own insufficient or ineffective insulin proteins.

> **DID YOU KNOW?**
>
> Modern insulin production relies upon genetically engineered bacteria. The bacteria have been engineered with a copy of the human insulin gene. The insulin-making bacteria can be grown inexpensively in vats. Before genetic engineering, insulin had to be purified from slaughtered pigs and cows. The animal insulin was expensive and time consuming to produce. Furthermore, people often developed antibodies to it because it is slightly different from human insulin. The immune system recognized the animal insulin as foreign and attacked it.

Gene therapy is the one of the great promises of genetic engineering. In theory, gene therapy inserts a "normal" copy of the "abnormal," or disease-causing, gene into the patient's DNA. The body's natural machinery then copies the gene, resulting in a normal protein. Function is restored, and the disease disappears.

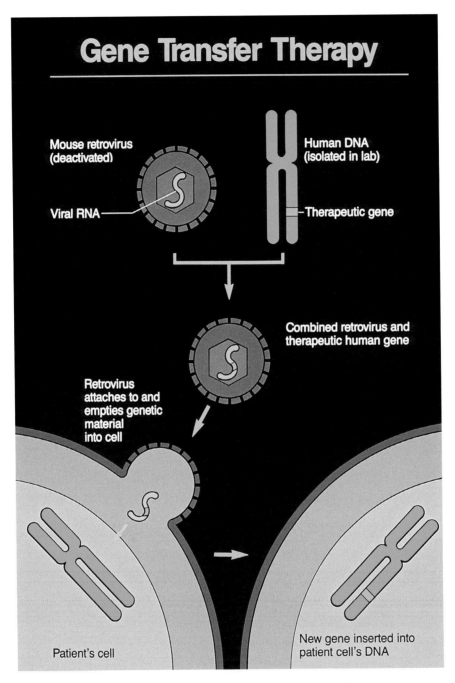

Gene Transfer Therapy

Mouse retrovirus
(deactivated)

Viral RNA

Human DNA
(isolated in lab)

Therapeutic gene

Combined retrovirus and
therapeutic human gene

Retrovirus
attaches to and
empties genetic
material
into cell

Patient's cell

New gene inserted into
patient cell's DNA

One type of gene therapy moves a therapeutic gene into a deactivated mouse virus. Retroviruses have the ability to insert their DNA into that of their host. Therefore, the retrovirus transfers the therapeutic gene into the patient's DNA, where it hopefully will be transcribed and translated into the therapeutic protein.

The first gene therapy trial began in 1990. Ashanthi DeSilva, a four-year-old girl, had a normally fatal disease called severe combined immune deficiency (SCID). Because of an abnormal gene, her body could not make an enzyme critical for the immune system: adenosine deaminase (ADA). As a result, she had lived her entire life quarantined from most people. For her gene therapy, doctors took some of her blood, including white blood cells. In the laboratory, they used a disabled virus to add a functional copy of the gene that makes ADA. They then returned the white blood cells to her body. Later, 30 percent of her white blood cells showed ADA production. Scientists and doctors were never completely able to say whether or not the gene therapy had worked, however, because Ashanthi was receiving other treatments at the same time. Later trials with different patients showed much poorer results.

As of 2013, no gene therapy products had been approved for sale in the United States. In fact, the only nation that has approved gene therapy treatments is China, where there are two drugs on the market for treatment of head and neck cancer. Researchers in the U.S. have had some successes, particularly in the treatment of immune disease. However, spectacular failures in some early trials make researchers and regulators very cautious about using genetic engineering. The potential is so great that research continues. Trials that employ genetic engineering to treat immune disease, liver cancer, hemophilia, and certain types of blindness have been under way for several years.

What else could genetic engineering do for human health? Scientists can envision growing new organs from a person's own stem cells

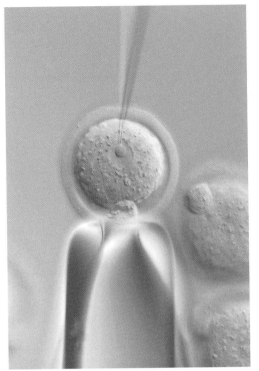

Stem cell research has great medical potential, but it ignites controversy.

to replace a damaged liver or spleen. Most cells can only make copies of themselves; so when an entire organ is damaged, the human body has no way to make a new copy of it.

New organs could theoretically be grown from a patient's own **stem cells**. A stem cell is one that retains its ability to produce different types of cells. Since the new organs would be grown from the patient's own cells, the issues of tissue rejection that all organ transplant recipients now face would not exist. However, scientists and doctors are only beginning to understand how to persuade adult stem cells to form entire organs outside (or inside) a body.

Efforts to grow organs or cells have transferred the nucleus from an adult cell and placed it in an egg from which the nucleus has been removed. Using chemical cues, the egg with its new nucleus divides in a test tube. Once the dividing cells have reached a critical point, stem cells, which have the ability to create many different types of tissues, can be removed. From this point on, with regard to disease therapies, human knowledge lags behind human aspiration. Knowing that adding retinoic acid to stem cells will lead to the formation of neurons does not constitute a therapy for Alzheimer's disease. Washing stem cells with serum albumin leads to the formation of white blood cells but falls far short of treating leukemia.

The **embryonic stem cell** research so often in the news relies upon a similar process whereby the dividing cells come from the union of sperm and egg instead of from an adult cell. Researchers have made more progress with stem cells when they originate from an embryo rather than from a chemically treated adult cell. For reasons not well understood, embryonic stem cells are more easily coaxed into different types of cells. Only recently have embryonic stem cell treatments for patients reached clinical trials. In 2010, the first trials focused on using embryonic stem cells for patients with spinal cord injuries. In 2011, doctors launched the second trials for helping patients with a particular type of blindness.

> **DID YOU KNOW?**
> Embryonic stem cells have been the source of great concern and debate. The debate hinges on how people view human embryos. In 2001, President George W. Bush limited the extent of embryonic stem cell research in the United States because of moral concerns having to do with the destruction of embryonic human life. In 2009, President Barack Obama removed many of the limitations because of the tremendous potential of embryonic stem cell therapies in medicine.

The techniques of genetic engineering may hold solutions for medical problems that we currently do not know how to solve. Today, patients can wait years for organ donors who are well matched. Even with careful matching, there is a high risk that a patient's body will reject the organ. Instead, patients waiting for an organ transplant could receive an organ grown from their own cells. For patients with genetic disease caused by a single missing or "broken" protein, simply replacing that one protein through gene therapy has the potential to completely cure the disorder.

To date, the promise of genetic engineering in medicine has not reached its potential. There have been some successful gene therapy trials. However, other spectacularly unsuccessful trials have made researchers, doctors, and patients very cautious. Stem cells have great potential to cure diseases and replace damaged tissues, even whole organs. Scientists and doctors, however, are only beginning to explore how to reach the potential of stem cells. In all of these cases, genetic engineering tools allow scientists and doctors to seek a new set of solutions. Since many of the solutions remain on the horizon, they have not yet reached the patients who need them.

Environmental Help: What Will Make the World a Better Place?

We live in a world that is increasingly polluted by the by-products of our lives. The food that we grow results in environmental contamination from pesticides. Meat and grain production yield high-nutrient run-off that can contaminate surface waters. Concentrated amounts of toxic substances such as mercury, oil, and other pollutants end up deposited in the environment, whether intentionally or unintentionally. Genetic engineering can contribute to solutions to many of these problems.

One of the most common genetic engineering practices today is the insertion of genes into crop plants to make the plants resistant to predators. Plants have been resisting pests naturally for centuries—the bitter taste of tea and the spicy taste of hot peppers is caused by plant defense proteins. One bacterium, called *Bacillus thuringiensis*, Bt for short, makes a protein called a *cry* protein. *Cry* proteins are fatal to many caterpillars and worms but have no effect at all on mammals (including humans). Organic farmers have been dusting Bt bacteria on their crops as a natural **pesticide** for many years. Genetic engineers took the *cry* gene out of the bacteria and transferred it into crops such as corn, soybeans, and cotton. Since farmers began planting insect-resistant corn and cotton around 1997, **insecticide** use in cotton production has declined. Insecticides are a type of pesticide used to kill insects. The decline in insecticide use may have also been influenced by other important factors, such as greater awareness of beneficial insects. Nevertheless, the data suggests that genetic engineering can positively impact the environment by reducing the amount of the often harsh chemical pesticides used in agriculture.

Plants and animals need nutrients such as nitrogen and phosphorus. To increase yields, farmers apply nitrogen- and phosphorus-containing fertilizer to their fields. Runoff from agricultural fields contains extra nutrients not taken up by the plants. Nitrogen and phosphorus are in short supply in natural systems, too. When a large pulse of phosphorus-rich runoff reaches a stream, pond, or ocean, it results in an increase of small photosynthetic organisms such as algae and phytoplankton. When these animals die, their decomposition consumes oxygen in the water; with too little oxygen, fish and other organisms cannot survive.

ENVIROPIGS

Pigs, like all other animals, need phosphorus to grow. Increasingly, pigs eat corn. Corn has plenty of phosphorus, but it is locked up in a compound called phytate. Neither pigs nor humans can unlock phytate to release and use the phosphorus. Therefore, pig farmers have to use expensive supplements to ensure that their pigs get enough phosphorus. Meanwhile, the phytate passes through the pigs and into waste lagoons, where it can be broken down by bacteria. These organisms have a gene that makes phytase. Phytase is an enzyme that breaks down phytate and thus makes the phosphorus available for use. Occasional spills or seepage from waste lagoons into groundwater release this "waste" phosphorus into ecosystems, where it can lead to algae blooms and deoxygenated waters.

Scientists and farmers have recently turned to genetic engineering for two solutions to the pig phosphorus problem. Plant breeders (with and without genetic engineering) have created low-phytase corn. The low-phytase corn reduces the runoff problem but still does not deliver phosphorus to the pig. What if there were a way for pigs to use the phytate in corn? It would be a win-win situation for the environment (less phosphorus pollution) and farmers (no more need for expensive phosphorus supplements for pigs). In 2001, genetic engineers moved a phytase gene from bacteria into the saliva of genetically engineered pigs. These pigs can extract nearly all the phosphorus they need from their feed, and they have 75 percent less phosphorus in their waste than nonengineered pigs.

Pollution of water and soil is a serious problem that goes beyond nutrients such as nitrogen and phosphorus. An important part of controlling pollution is being able to measure it. Air pollution can be measured with relative ease. However, measuring pollutants in water is not as easy. In the same way that miners used canaries to detect dangerous gases in coal mines, scientists are using genetically engineered organisms to help detect signs of danger in water. Recently scientists engineered the transparent zebra fish to glow in the presence of pollutants such as heavy metals, estrogen-like compounds, or insecticides. The fish are intended for use in test tanks, not in natural ecosystems. In a similar way, genetically engineered mustard plants can be used to detect explosives and the chemicals benzene and xylene.

Other plants go a step further and can collect or decontaminate toxic waste containing heavy metals. For example, scientists at the University of Georgia have engineered mustard plants with two bacterial genes to convert dangerous mercury compounds in the soil into much less harmful elemental mercury. Other plants and algae are planned to

Transparent zebra fish have been engineered with a green flourescent protein and will glow in the presence of environmental contaminents like heavy metals.

help decontaminate soils containing arsenic, lead, and other harmful pollutants. Using plants to restore a polluted environment, a process known as **phytoremediation**, is often a cheaper, easier alternative to removing and chemically cleaning soils.

Genetic engineering has the potential to solve some environmental problems. Agricultural plants can be engineered to resist pests; such plants would reduce the need for toxic chemical pesticides. Crops can be tailored to better fit the nutritional needs of the animals consuming them. This tailoring reduces the nutrient content of runoff and downstream negative effects on rivers, lakes, and oceans. Furthermore, plants can be engineered to identify, catch, and even detoxify pollutants in soil and water. Animals can be engineered to signal when waters are polluted, and so environmental problems can be identified before they become disasters.

Through the modification of plants and animals, the tools and techniques of genetic engineering have the potential to positively impact human lives. Engineering plants and animals can lead to a larger and more nutritious food supply for the growing world population. Human health can be directly improved by genetically engineered plants that can make vaccines or by genetically engineered bacteria that can grow proteins for medicines. The prospects of using gene therapy to replace "broken" genes or using cloned organs for transplant have great potential for changing medicine and saving lives. Some of these techniques, such as engineering crop plants and bacteria, are already widespread. Others remain promises on the horizon.

WHAT DO YOU THINK?

Is growing transgenic papaya a good idea? Who benefits from it? What are the potential risks? What additional information do you need to make a good decision?

Is consuming golden rice a good idea? Who benefits from it? What are the potential risks? What additional information do you need to make a good decision?

Is using gene therapy a good idea? Who benefits from it? What are the potential risks? What additional information do you need to make a good decision?

Is using adult stem cells to grow organs for transplant patients a good idea? Who benefits from it? What are the potential risks? What additional information do you need to make a good decision?

Is using embryonic stem cells a good idea? Who benefits from it? What are the potential risks? What additional information do you need to make a good decision?

Is phytoremediation, the use of plants to clean up the environment, a good idea? Who benefits from it? What are the potential risks? What additional information do you need to make a good decision?

To reduce the amount of phosphate runoff from corn-fed pigs, do you think scientists should engineer the plants, the pigs, both, or neither? Why?

Chapter 3

Despite the promise of genetic engineering, such new tools can bring unexpected new dangers. History is full of examples of the unintended consequences of technology. The pesticide DDT was originally greeted as a wonderful chemical because it reduced malaria, a debilitating disease, by killing mosquitoes. Decades later, California condors were on the verge of extinction because the long-lived DDT residues had accumulated in the bodies of the animals, and they could no longer reproduce. The United States has banned DDT for agricultural use, though some countries still use it for malaria control, and condor populations are slowly recovering. The story serves as a warning about the unintended consequences of apparently beneficial technology.

Unintended Consequences

What are the likely unintended consequences of genetic engineering? We cannot know the answer to this question because genetic engineering forces us to deal with situations we have never encountered before. We cannot know the health effects of regular consumption of genetically modified foods. Nor can we know exactly how gene therapy will affect those treated. Regulatory agencies must wrestle with

Some people choose to eat organic foods to avoid consumption of genetically engineered plants.

the question of whether crop plants that produce a pesticide should be treated as crops or as pesticides. All of these situations are new. However, we can anticipate some of the areas where the risk of unintended consequences is fairly high. The following are some possible areas of concern:

- the health effects of genetically modified food for the consumer
- unexpected problems in gene therapies
- the ecological consequences of genes "escaping" into nontarget organisms
- the evolution of resistance to genetically modified plants

As a society, we will have to decide whether the potential and largely unknown risks of genetic engineering outweigh the potential and often theoretical benefits.

HEALTH EFFECTS AND ALLERGIES

What happens when you take a gene from an almond tree and move it to a cabbage plant? Can someone with a nut allergy still safely eat cabbage? Allergic reactions are one troubling unknown with genetically modified organisms (**GMOs**). As a result, regulatory agencies such as the Environmental Protection Agency (EPA) and the Food and Drug Administration (FDA) have been cautious about what they approve for human consumption. A genetically engineered product goes through testing before it is approved.

Additional unintended health effects could come from antibiotic resistance genes used as part of the genetic engineering process. Such genes are important to screen for successful incorporation of engineered genes, but continue to be made by the engineered plant or animal throughout its life. Some scientists fear that antibiotic resistance genes could interfere with digestion of prescribed antibiotics in a sick individual. People also worry about unlikely, but potentially serious, transfer of these antibiotic resistance genes to disease-causing bacteria. Scientists have recently developed several other screening techniques that decrease reliance upon antibiotic resistance in response to concerns.

PROBLEMS WITH GENE THERAPY

Although gene therapy holds promise for curing diseases, there are still many problems to be worked out. Some problems are dangerous. Other problems merely make gene therapy short-lived, ineffective, or expensive.

To be a permanent solution, gene therapy must insert a normal copy of a gene into cells in a stable, long-lived way. Engineered cells will go on to produce daughter cells with the new, normal gene. For reasons we do not understand, engineered genes often end up in unstable locations and thus are ineffective. Therefore, many rounds of expensive therapy are often necessary for successful gene therapy.

Finding a way to safely deliver genes into cells remains a persistent problem. To date, most efforts have focused on using viruses as vectors to carry a normal copy of a gene into cells that contain a disease-causing gene. Before use, the virus is disabled; that is, critical disease-causing genes are inactivated. But disabled viruses can still cause immune reactions—in such cases, the body recognizes the virus as "foreign," fights it, and in so doing, kills critical cells. Depending on the size and scale, immune reactions to virus vectors can prove fatal.

Other problems with using viruses include toxicity, inflammation, and control over where the gene inserts into the cell. Scientists are working on other techniques that do not require viruses to deliver genes into cells.

MOVEMENT OF GENES

Engineering a gene into a plant is no guarantee that it is going to remain there. Plants have many mechanisms to move their genes around, in spite of being anchored to the ground. Stationary plants rely on wind, insects, birds, and bats to move their pollen. Cross-pollination is an important part of many plants' survival. The genetically engineered pollen blowing in the wind contains engineered genes, and if it pollinates a nonengineered plant, the resulting seeds have a 50 percent chance of receiving the engineered gene. This movement of genes is also called **transgenic escape** or **horizontal gene transfer**. Engineered genes of cross-pollinated plants can be expected to move into the next generation of seeds and plants. For example, genetically engineered corn pollen may travel miles to fertilize other corn plants. At least some of the resulting seeds will have the engineered genes.

Transfer of genes from one corn plant to another should not be a surprise. However, in 2001 and again in 2009, scientists detected engineered genes in the traditional varieties of corn found in Mexican farm fields. The news was surprising because the Mexican government had prohibited the planting of genetically engineered corn varieties in order to protect diverse, traditional types of corn and prevent such transfer. Scientists are still arguing about the methods used for detection, but it seems inevitable that genetically engineered pollen will reach and fertilize nonengineered plants if they are nearby.

Though engineered pollen moves freely from one corn plant to another, many genetic engineering advocates have argued that engineered genes are unlikely to escape crops and create so-called **superweeds**. To create a superweed, pollen must reach and fertilize a weedy, wild plant relative and result in the formation of a seed. The seed must grow into a plant containing the engineered gene. The plant must survive and reproduce and so pass the engineered gene along to its offspring.

For the rare engineered gene to increase in a plant population, it must give the host some advantage over its neighbors. Then, over generations natural selection will cause the gene to increase in the population. This combination of events might seem impossibly rare, but it has already occurred.

The canola plant, from which canola oil is extracted, grows alongside its relative, wild mustard, in the United States and Canada. Much of the canola crop has been engineered to contain a gene

Pollen from flowering canola plants can cross-pollinate nearby wild mustard plants, particularly in the northern United States and Canada. By this mechanism, genetically engineered genes can move from the crop to the wild, weedy relative.

for **herbicide** resistance. Herbicides are used to kill weeds. Farmers can spray a field of herbicide-resistant crops and kill all the weeds without hurting the crop. In 2010, a report showed that 86 percent of wild mustard plants sampled along roads in North Dakota contained an engineered gene for resistance to common herbicides. This could pose long-term problems for people, particularly farmers, who spray herbicides to eliminate weeds.

EVOLUTION OF RESISTANCE

Plants and their insect predators are engaged in a battle for survival. Plants evolve defenses to the predators that eat them. A plant with a good defense, whether natural or genetically engineered, gives the plant a strong advantage. Therefore, the plant is more likely to pass its genes along to the next generation. In subsequent generations, advantageous genes can quickly spread throughout a population. The evolutionary advantage falls to the insect that happens to be invulnerable to the new plant defense. The invulnerable insect now has a strong evolutionary advantage and is highly likely to pass its genes on to the next generation. The invulnerable gene quickly moves through the insect population. Over the centuries, plants develop defenses, and insects overcome them. Genetic engineering allows new ways to defend plants. But insect populations remain under strong evolutionary pressure to overcome those defenses.

Remember the cases of cotton and corn plants engineered to contain genes from the *Bacillus thuringiensis* bacteria? Plants containing these Bt genes make their own pesticide—a *cry* protein that is fatal to many caterpillars and worms. However, if pests such as the cotton bollworm (*Helicoverpa zea*) and the fall armyworm (*Spodoptera frugiperda*) can somehow resist the plant defenses, they have a major advantage over other worms. A vulnerable worm will likely die. A resistant worm will survive and pass its special, naturally occurring resistance genes along to its offspring. Very quickly, a population of resistant worms will arise.

Cotton genetically engineered to resist the cotton bollworm has reduced pesticide use, but could be fertile ground for evolution of resistance to the engineered genes.

Who Benefits?

Major agricultural seed and chemical companies developed most of the genetically engineered products on the market. Farmers pay a premium for genetically engineered crop varieties presumably because they offer an economic benefit—usually they save labor and reduce the need for pesticides. Most herbicide-tolerant and pest-resistant Bt varieties on the market have no benefit to consumers beyond potentially reduced food costs. They help farmers by reducing weeding and insect problems in the field. They benefit chemical companies that sell more herbicides to spray on herbicide-resistant fields. In this way, most of the genetically engineered agricultural crops on the market continue the last century's trend of increasing reliance on oil-based chemicals for increased food production.

Not surprisingly, some consumers have been opposed to eating genetically engineered foods. Europeans and Japanese have been so opposed that they allow few agricultural imports from the United States, in order to avoid genetically engineered foods. Opponents see few benefits and potential risks from a new technology. Genetically modified crops are present in the majority (at least 70 percent) of processed food, yet their presence is unlabeled. In many polls, the vast majority of Americans favor labeling of genetically engineered foods; proportions of people favoring labeling ranged from 58 to 87 percent. Many other nations, including the European Union, require labeling of genetically engineered foods. Though several U.S. state, local and national legislatures have introduced genetically engineered food labeling bills, none have passed. Companies that produce genetically engineered crops and processed foods are among the strongest opponents to labeling because of the costs of changing labels and fears of consumers rejecting genetically engineered products.

Is Regulation Adequate?

Governments around the world regulate genetically modified organisms. Some regulation is intended to protect the consumer from dangerous food or drug products. Other regulation aims to protect the environment and or agricultural resources. In addition, governments also regulate **genetic modification** due to ethical concerns, as in the case of embryonic stem cell research.

Who is in charge of monitoring and regulating genetically engineered organisms? Are they being tested, monitored, and regulated adequately? These are not simple questions to answer. Instead of creating new regulatory structures for genetically engineered organisms, as the European Union did, the U.S. government has extended standards and definitions already in place for nonengineered products. For example, if a plant produces a genetically engineered pesticide, as Bt crops do, should it be regulated as a plant? Or should it be regulated as a pesticide?

In reality, in the United States different government agencies regulate different aspects of a genetically engineered organism. The three major agencies involved in regulating genetically engineered organisms are the USDA (United States Department of Agriculture), the EPA (Environmental Protection Agency), and the FDA (Food and Drug Administration). The USDA is responsible for protecting against threats such as weeds, disease, and pests. For example, the USDA has studied and developed guidelines for minimizing development of Bt resistance and superweeds. The EPA is responsible for ensuring safe pesticide use and regulating the use of new microorganisms. The EPA registers and sets limits for the use of pesticides, such as Bt, even when produced by plants. The FDA is responsible for the safety of food and animal feed. The FDA was responsible for determining whether herbicide-resistant soybeans were safe for human consumption.

Activists advocate the labeling of genetically engineered food.

The resulting web of definitions is so complex and technical that many experts have trouble understanding it. Are genetically engineered food products being adequately tested in this complex system? For example, the FDA does not do independent testing of genetically engineered products. Such testing would be expensive and complicated. Instead the FDA relies on companies to provide safety data about their products. Even if an engineered protein is thought to be safe, testing occurs on adults, not children, babies, or pregnant women.

Playing God?

Many people are fundamentally uncomfortable with our new ability to alter organisms. Genetic engineering enables us to move genes across species barriers. Where is the ethical line at which people become uncomfortable? In studies commissioned by the Pew Initiative on Food and **Biotechnology** in 2003 to explore Americans' attitudes and understanding about genetically engineered products, Americans were more comfortable with the genetic engineering of plants than of animals, and they were fully 4.5 times more comfortable when the process was applied to plants rather than humans.

In another Pew survey from 2006, a majority of people (61 percent) were uncomfortable with the idea of cloning animals, and only 22 percent believed that food from cloned animals would be safe. Between 2001 and 2006, the percentage of people favoring introduction of genetically engineered food into U.S. food supplies declined from 58 to 46 percent, while the percentage of those supporting it remained stable at around 27 percent. Interestingly, more than 50 percent of people reported that they were unlikely to eat genetically modified food, even though anyone eating nonorganic corn or soy products eats genetically modified foods.

WHAT DO YOU THINK?

Would you eat genetically engineered food? (An estimated 70 percent of processed foods at the grocery store contain genetically modified corn, soy, or canola.)

Would you wear clothes made from genetically altered cotton?

Do you think human cloning is a good idea? What are the risks involved? What are the benefits?

What are some of the ecological dangers of planting genetically engineered crops?

Decisions about whether or not to use genetic engineering are not simple. Each decision has complex trade-offs and consequences. Consider the cases below, and you decide. Is genetic engineering a good idea?

SCIDding into Gene Therapy?

You are the parent of a four-year-old child named Jason. Jason has a severe, usually fatal disease called severe combined immune deficiency (SCID). Jason's body cannot make a critical enzyme called adenosine deaminase (ADA) because the gene that encodes it is abnormal and nonfunctional. Without ADA, Jason's immune system does not function. This means that he is vulnerable to every germ that he is exposed to. His body has no way to defend itself. Jason has lived his entire life in a "bubble"—a protective plastic enclosure that isolates him from exposure to germs. Even a kiss from you, his parent, would put his life at risk.

Jason's doctor has heard about a gene therapy trial to treat ADA. The trial uses a disabled virus to transfer a normal copy of the gene that encodes ADA. This is the gene that is causing Jason's problems.

Scientists analyze the genes of Eastern grass for genes that enable it to tolerate flooding. If found, the genes could be transferred to other crops, like corn, to create flood-tolerant varieties.

Gene therapy for SCIDs has shown some success. The first case of gene therapy was a SCID case. Ashanthi DeSilva, in 1990, had some blood cells removed from her body; they were treated and then returned. Unlike Ashanthi's treatment, Jason's would take place inside his body; a disabled virus would be used to carry the normal gene into his cells. His treatment, if successful, would have a higher probability of being permanent.

Treatments using viruses have had problems in the past. Patients can have an immune reaction to the virus—that is, the body's immune system can attempt to destroy or expel it. Such a reaction is especially unlikely in Jason's case since his immune system is already so weak that its capacity to resist any invader is small. He could also have reactions leading to severe inflammation, toxicity, and death. You, as his parent, may have some misgivings about changing his DNA. But if you do nothing, Jason will likely die of some sort of infection before reaching adulthood.

You decide. Will you use genetic engineering to treat Jason?

What's for Lunch?

You go to the grocery store to choose your foods for the week. What do you

Ashanthi DeSilva received gene therapy for severe combined immune deficiency (SCID).

choose? Do you choose to eat genetically engineered foods? Are you willing to eat the Bt proteins that are deadly to caterpillars? Research shows that Bt proteins are safe for humans because humans digest their food with stomach acid, while caterpillars use a totally different mechanism.

Genetically engineered canned food.

Each year, there are more and more genetically engineered foods on the market, and they are not labeled as genetically engineered. In the United States, you can assume that any product that contains corn or soy has been genetically engineered. The list of products includes cereal, soda, and many kinds of candy. The only way to avoid genetically engineered foods is to eat foods labeled organic or GMO-free.

What are you willing to eat? The FDA has declared genetically engineered foods safe for humans to eat. Do you think their testing is adequate? Their tests are for adults. Do you trust the results for small children or babies? Would you allow your child to eat genetically engineered foods?

Do you think the answers would be the same if you lived in a place where food is scarce? For example, if you lived in a famine-struck part of Africa where the soil was too salty or dry to grow crops from nonengineered seed, would you be willing to eat genetically engineered food that could be grown under such conditions?

What Is in Your Field?

You are a canola farmer in Nebraska with a small farm—one of the few left in your county. It's planting time, and you need to decide which seeds to buy. Last year you had terrible problems with weeds. To combat them, you had to do a lot of cultivation with your tractor, which takes time and a lot of gasoline. And gas is expensive these days! You could pull the weeds by hand, but it would take weeks that you simply do not have.

Wind can carry genetically engineered pollen, resulting in unintentional fertilization of organic crops.

Are you interested in buying herbicide-resistant seeds? With these seeds, you can spray the field with an herbicide such as Round-up or Liberty, and the weeds will die while the canola survives. Genetically engineered seeds are more expensive than regular seeds. You have to buy the herbicide, too. But it is likely to save you time and reduce your fuel costs.

You should not have any trouble finding a buyer for the genetically engineered canola. Once you sell your harvest at the local buyers co-op, it is mixed with nonengineered canola. It is all processed together. (Organic canola is an exception. Organic foods are usually separated from the nonorganic harvest.)

Your neighbor is an organic farmer. She grows canola too. She is very worried about the pollen from genetically engineered plants in your fields blowing onto her organic canola crop. The harvested seeds from her plants would then contain some genetically engineered genes. If that happens, she wonders will her organic canola still qualify as organic?

A recent study showed that most of the weedy mustard plants in Nebraska have resistance to the same herbicides sprayed on canola. Herbicide would not kill those weeds if they ended up in the field. Then again, most of your weed problems do not come from wild mustard. Are you worried about herbicide-resistant weeds that would defeat the purpose of buying the genetically engineered seeds? Are you worried about planting herbicide-resistant seeds and making the wild mustard problem worse in your state?

You decide. What kind of seeds will you buy?

Toxic Cleanup

You are the site manager for a former landfill. Decades' worth of garbage has left the ground contaminated with heavy metals such as lead, mercury, and cadmium. You have to decide how to clean up the site before it can be used.

One option is to use bulldozers to scrape off all the contaminated soil. In addition to the expense of this process, there is the problem of deciding what to do with the contaminated soil.

Another solution is to use genetically engineered plants to capture or convert some of the toxic waste. For example, you could use a mustard plant that has been engineered to convert the highly toxic methyl mercury to much less harmful forms and release them as gas. Would you be willing to use the genetically engineered mercury-converting plants?

Your site is in an area where wild mustard plants grow. The pollen from the genetically engineered plants might reach the wild mustard and transfer the mercury-converting genes. Is that a problem?

Other genetically engineered plants have been designed to capture heavy metals in their plant tissues. This is a good way to remove the metals from your site. But what do you do with the heavy-metal-containing plants once they have captured the metals from the soil? If you throw them out, you might just be putting the metals back into a landfill. Instead, those plants require special processing to make sure that the heavy metals end up somewhere safe.

Would you be willing to use genetically engineered microorganisms? A natural soil bacterium, *Deinococcus radiodurans*, has been engineered to contain mercury-converting genes. Like the mustard plants, it takes harmful forms of mercury and converts them to less toxic forms that are released as gas. Would you be willing to release the bacteria in your site? Once you have released it, there is no way to recapture it. Do you worry about it mutating? Do you worry about it transferring its genes to other bacteria?

You decide. Which, if any, of these genetically engineered tools are you willing to use to clean up your toxic site?

Glossary

artificial selection—The selection of organisms for a desirable set of characteristics. The process mimics natural selection but is driven by human goals and actions, rather than by "survival of the fittest."

asexual reproduction—The creation of two (or more) genetically identical individuals by dividing, budding, taking plant cuttings, or other means that do not involve sexual recombination of genes.

biotechnology—Any application of technology to biology. Genetic engineering is biotechnology. Other examples of biotechnology include medical technologies like vaccination or use of microorganisms in fermentation of food and drink.

chromosome—A long, tightly wound string of DNA that carries all or most of the genes of an organism.

clone—A genetically identical copy of a gene, genetic sequence, or individual. Scientists clone genes to learn about them.

DNA—Deoxyribonucleic acid, the material of which genes are made. DNA has four bases (A, T, G, and C) that pair with one another.

double helix—Two strands of DNA bases paired with each other to form a twisting ladder where genetic information is encoded on one strand and backed up on the other. This structure is highly stable and helps to protect organisms from harmful mutations.

embryonic stem cell—A cell from the union of a sperm and egg that has the ability to produce different types of cells and tissues.

gene—A functional, heritable segment of DNA that encodes proteins.

gene therapy—Replacement of an abnormal, disease-causing gene with a "normal," functioning copy of the same gene.

genetic engineering—The process of making intentional, direct change to an organism's DNA.

genetic modification—Alteration of an organism's genetic material by direct or indirect means.

genome—All the genetic material within an organism.

GMO—A genetically modified (more precisely, genetically engineered) organism. GMOs are usually plants that have been genetically engineered with DNA from other organisms.

herbicide—A chemical or compound used to kill weeds.

horizontal gene transfer—The movement of genes from one, intended species to another, unintentional species. The process is also known as transgenic escape.

insecticide—A chemical or compound used to kill (or repel) insects.

mutation—A significant and relatively permanent change in DNA, typically involving the physical alteration of the organism affected.

natural selection—The mechanism by which evolution occurs in nature. The individuals that have the most offspring increase the frequency of their genes and traits in the next generation. Over time, the most "fit" genes and traits become the most prevalent.

nucleus—The membrane-bound compartment inside a plant or animal cell that holds DNA.

pesticide—A chemical or compound, usually made from oil, used to kill or repel pests, including insects, fungi, and rodents.

phytoremediation—The process of using plants to restore a polluted environment.

protein—A compound constructed from a genetic template. Proteins contribute to the formation of muscles, digestive and other enzymes, immune-defense antibodies, and other tissue structures.

stem cell—An unspecialized cell that retains its ability to produce different types of cells and tissues.

superweed—A weed that has acquired (unintentionally) genetically engineered genes that give it an ecological advantage. For example, canola plants with resistance to herbicides can pass the resistance gene to a nearby weed.

transgenic escape—The movement of genes from one, intended species to another, unintentional species. The process is also known as horizontal gene transfer.

Find Out More

Books

Cohen, Marina. *Genetic Engineering: Can We Improve on Nature?* (Let's Relate to Genetics). St. Catharines, ON: Crabtree, 2010.

Hodge, Russ. *Genetic Engineering: Manipulating the Mechanisms of Life*. New York: Facts on File, 2009.

Jones, Phill. *Stem Cell Research and Other Cell-Related Controversies*. New York: Chelsea House Publishing, 2011.

Simpson, Kathleen. *National Geographic Investigates: Genetics: From DNA to Designer Dogs*. Washington, DC: National Geographic Society, 2008.

Yount, Lisa. *Biotechnology and Genetic Engineering* (Library in a Book). New York: Facts on File, 2008.

Websites

Adoption of Genetically Engineered Crops in the U.S.: Extent of Adoption

www.ers.usda.gov/data/biotechcrops/adoption.htm

Figures demonstrate the rising areas of genetically engineered crops in the United States.

Embryonic Stem Cell Research: An Ethical Dilemma

www.eurostemcell.org/factsheet/embyronic-stem-cell-research-ethical-dilemma

This website discusses the ethical dilemma of stem cell research and why the arguments are difficult to resolve.

Human Genome Project Information: Gene Therapy

www.ornl.gov/sci/techresources/Human_Genome/medicine/genetherapy.shtml

The website gives an overview of gene therapy, how it works, and recent developments in research.

Millennium Development Goals of the United Nations

www.un.org/millenniumgoals/poverty.shtml

This website contains the developmental goals of the United Nation. Pay particular attention to Goal 1: Eradicate Extreme Poverty and Hunger.

Report to the Pew Initiative on Food and Biotechnology: Review of Public Opinion Research

www.pewtrusts.org/news_room_detail.aspx?id=32802

This report analyzes the attitudes about genetic engineering after recent studies found that the public understanding of genetically modified food remains low.

Reproductive Cloning Pro and Con Arguments

www.geneticsandsociety.org/article.php?id=282

This webpage contains pro and con arguments as well as corresponding rebuttals on the topic of human reproductive cloning.

Research Ethics and Stem Cells

http://stemcells.nih.gov/info/ethics.asp

As science and technology continue to advance, there is a corresponding increase in ethical viewpoints surrounding these developments. This site analyzes the ethical viewpoints on stem cell research.

World Population Database

http://esa.un.org/unpd/wpp/Excel-Data/population.htm

The United Nations produces this website full of information about world population.

Index

Page numbers in boldface are illustrations.

About the Author

Elizabeth Rice is an adjunct professor of biology at Franklin and Marshall College, in Lancaster, Pennsylvania. She is also the assistant director of the bioinformatics program. She earned her doctorate from Cornell University while studying corn genetics and conservation of genetic diversity in Mexico. She enjoys gardening, hiking, cooking, sewing, and following her two small children on their adventures.